# What Is the Story of Looney Tunes™?

# What Is the Story of Looney Tunes™?

by Steve Korté

illustrated by John Hinderliter

Penguin Workshop

In memory of my brother Paul
and our many happy Saturday mornings
watching Bugs Bunny and his pals—SK

For Finn and Javi, may they always
be kids at heart—JH

PENGUIN WORKSHOP
An Imprint of Penguin Random House LLC, New York

Published by Penguin Workshop, an imprint of Penguin Random House LLC, New York. PENGUIN and PENGUIN WORKSHOP are trademarks of Penguin Books Ltd. WHO HQ & Design is a registered trademark of Penguin Random House LLC. Printed in the USA.

Visit us online at www.penguinrandomhouse.com.

Library of Congress Control Number: 2019034729

ISBN 9781524788360 (paperback)          10 9 8 7 6 5 4 3 2 1
ISBN 9781524788377 (library binding)     10 9 8 7 6 5 4 3 2 1

# Contents

What Is the Story of Looney Tunes? . . . . . . . . 1

Drawings That Move . . . . . . . . . . . . . . . . . . 4

Launching Looney Tunes . . . . . . . . . . . . . 18

"Th-th-that's All, Folks!" . . . . . . . . . . . . . . . 24

A Very Daffy Duck . . . . . . . . . . . . . . . . . . 34

"What's Up, Doc?" . . . . . . . . . . . . . . . . . . 45

New Arrivals . . . . . . . . . . . . . . . . . . . . . 57

"Beep! Beep!" . . . . . . . . . . . . . . . . . . . . 64

The Best of the Best . . . . . . . . . . . . . . . . . 71

TV Stars . . . . . . . . . . . . . . . . . . . . . . . . 82

Loonier Than Ever . . . . . . . . . . . . . . . . . . 88

Bibliography . . . . . . . . . . . . . . . . . . . . . 106

# What Is the Story of Looney Tunes?

Across America in October of 1937, adults and kids settled in to their theater seats to enjoy a feature film from the Warner Bros. movie studio. Before the feature film, they watched the coming attractions and a short movie with news events from around the world. There was also a black-and-white cartoon called *Rover's Rival*. The star of the cartoon was a small, plump pig named Porky. He was dressed in only a jacket and bowtie, and he stuttered when he spoke.

*Rover's Rival* begins with Porky Pig reading a book called *New Tricks to Teach Your Dog*. Porky is determined to teach his old dog, Rover, some of those new tricks. Sadly, Rover is so old that he can barely move or even hear what Porky is saying. But then a new puppy comes along who is eager to please Porky. Unfortunately, a game of fetch goes wrong when the puppy retrieves several lit sticks of dynamite and delivers them to Porky. It's up to Rover to grab the dynamite and move it far away from Porky before it explodes. Rover saves the day, and the story ends happily.

But that wasn't the end of the cartoon. In the closing seconds, as music played in the background, the screen was filled with the image of a giant drum that was labeled "Looney Tunes." Suddenly, Porky Pig burst through the drum! Movie audiences jumped in their seats. With a wave of his hand, Porky stammered, "Th-th-that's all, folks!"

It was at this moment that Porky Pig became a star. And the "Looney Tunes" went on to become some of the funniest and most beloved cartoons of all time.

# CHAPTER 1
## Drawings That Move

Animated movies are a series of filmed images—sometimes drawings and sometimes objects, such as clay models. When the filmed images are shown quickly one after another, it appears that they are moving. Short animated movies are also known as cartoons, and they have been around since the late 1800s.

In 1906, the Vitagraph movie studio released the first American animated cartoon. It was a three-minute silent film called *Humorous Phases of Funny Faces*. It showed a series of drawings that somehow seemed to come to life, including the faces of a man and woman smiling and frowning. The drawings weren't fancy, and there wasn't much of a story. But this cartoon inspired other artists to try and create new animated films.

One of those artists was a newspaper cartoonist named Winsor McCay. In 1914, he created the first cartoon character to become a star. The name of the cartoon was *Gertie the Dinosaur*,

and its star was a giant brontosaurus named Gertie. McCay made more than five thousand drawings to create just this one cartoon.

Winsor McCay

# Movie Shorts

A trip to a movie theater in the late 1920s cost around twenty-five cents. In those days audiences would watch a feature film and several short films, called "shorts." Those short films were between five and ten minutes long and would often include a comedy, news stories from around the world, a travel story, or a cartoon.

When television arrived in the late 1940s, movie shorts started to disappear from movie theaters. But many decades-old cartoons and other types of movie shorts found new life on television. A whole new generation of viewers was introduced to the stars of movie shorts from another era, including Laurel and Hardy, the Three Stooges, and the Little Rascals.

The advertisements for *Gertie* read, "She eats, drinks, and breathes. She laughs and cries. Dances the tango. Answers questions and obeys every command. Yet she lived millions of years before man inhabited the earth and has never been seen since!"

During her cartoon, Gertie bows to the audience, gobbles down a tree, and plays with a woolly mammoth. Audiences fell in love with Gertie. And McCay's cartoon inspired a whole generation of artists to create even more amazing animated films.

When many people think of animated movies, they think of Walt Disney. Although Disney did not invent animated films, his movie studio came up with new ideas that changed the way cartoons were made. In 1919, when Disney decided to become an artist and form his own advertising company, he and another artist named Ub Iwerks began making short animated movies.

Walt Disney (left)  and Ub Iwerks

11

They created a series of *Alice in Wonderland* cartoons that were somewhat successful, and the Disney animation studio grew to include more artists. Walt Disney found his first big success in 1927 when he released a cartoon starring Oswald the Lucky Rabbit. Oswald was a big hit, but a year later, Disney had an even bigger hit. His new character had round ears and a long, thin tail. His name was Mickey Mouse.

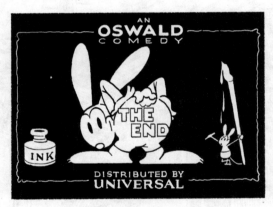

Oswald the Lucky Rabbit

In 1928, Mickey changed the very nature of cartoons. That was the year he starred in *Steamboat Willie*, the first animated cartoon with talking characters. Not only did Mickey speak, but audiences also heard sound effects and music in the cartoon.

Before 1927, movies were filmed without sound. Instead of spoken words, written dialogue would appear on the screen. When the movies were shown in theaters, live music would usually be provided by a piano player or sometimes a full orchestra. That changed when the Warner brothers—Harry, Albert, Sam, and Jack—released a feature film with sound called *The Jazz Singer* from their movie studio, Warner Bros. Pictures.

# Walt Disney (1901–1966)

Walt Disney always said that his two happiest childhood memories were his years growing up on a farm and whenever he found time to draw. Years later he found a way to combine those two happy memories. That's when he became an animation artist and created a series of cartoons featuring a whole farmyard's worth of memorable animal characters, including a mouse, a duck, a dog, and three little pigs.

Walt Disney produced the first sound cartoon, the first full-color cartoon, and the first feature-length animated movie. For four decades, he personally produced dozens of beloved movies and television series. He also launched two popular theme parks, Disneyland and Walt Disney World. Walt Disney is now widely recognized as one of the most important people in the history of animated films.

"Partners"

"We believe in our ideas: a family park where
parents and children could have fun · together."
Walt Disney

The movie starred a famous actor and singer named Al Jolson, who could be heard speaking and singing for the first time in a movie. Audiences went wild for what were then called "talking pictures" and demanded more of them. Almost immediately, silent movies disappeared and were replaced by ones with recorded voices, sound effects, and music.

The sound technology of *The Jazz Singer* changed movies forever. And with Mickey Mouse leading the way, sound cartoons were about to explode in popularity.

# CHAPTER 2
## Launching Looney Tunes

Adding sound to animation made Mickey Mouse into a worldwide movie superstar. But Walt Disney and his animators weren't content with Mickey's success. They wanted each new cartoon to look better than the last one.

The Disney artists created several more popular characters, including Donald Duck, Goofy, and Pluto. In 1929, the studio launched a series they called "Silly Symphony" that did not feature Mickey or any of the other popular characters. The first cartoon in this series was *The Skeleton Dance*, a cartoon of four human skeletons dancing around a graveyard. *Flowers and Trees*, the first full-color Silly Symphony cartoon, came out in 1932.

In 1937, Disney stunned the movie industry by releasing the first full-length animated feature film, *Snow White and the Seven Dwarfs*. It was Disney's biggest success to date.

Other movie studios had watched Disney's success and launched their own animated cartoons and cartoon series. Movie theaters now had plenty of cartoons to show, starring Popeye the Sailor, Betty Boop, Krazy Kat, and dozens of other characters.

Warner Bros. Pictures didn't have an animation studio of their own, but after the success of *The Jazz Singer*, they wanted to make cartoons, too.

They made a deal with a movie producer named Leon Schlesinger to create a series of cartoons with sound that would be called "Looney Tunes." Mr. Schlesinger didn't know a thing about making cartoons, so he hired two former Disney animators named Hugh Harman and Rudolf Ising. The two men created a cheerful cartoon character named Bosko. With the help of a few more artists, they soon had a cartoon ready for Warner Bros. It was *Sinkin' in the Bathtub*, and when it was released in 1930, audiences loved it.

Warner Bros. was so happy with the success of *Sinkin' in the Bathtub* that they rushed to make more Looney Tunes cartoons. The studio also added a second series called "Merrie Melodies."

Warner Bros. was now determined to become Disney's biggest competitor.

# Leon Schlesinger (1884–1949)

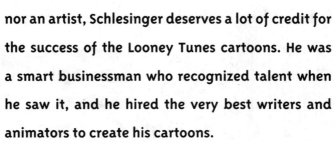

The movie producer Leon Schlesinger got his start working in stage theaters as an usher, actor, agent, and manager. Although he was neither a writer nor an artist, Schlesinger deserves a lot of credit for the success of the Looney Tunes cartoons. He was a smart businessman who recognized talent when he saw it, and he hired the very best writers and animators to create his cartoons.

From 1930 through 1944, he was the producer of Warner Bros. Looney Tunes and Merrie Melodies cartoons.

# CHAPTER 3
## "Th-th-that's All, Folks!"

Audiences loved the Looney Tunes and Merrie Melodies cartoons. Leon Schlesinger and Warner Bros. were happy. The only two people who were unhappy were animators Hugh Harman and Rudolf Ising. They wanted to earn more money and have bigger budgets for their cartoons.

In 1933, they asked for a raise, but Mr. Schlesinger turned them down. As a result, the two animators quit and took Bosko and the other characters they had created with them.

Rudolf Ising (left) and Hugh Harman

Warner Bros. still owned the series names Looney Tunes and Merrie Melodies, but they didn't have any characters to put in those cartoons! Schlesinger hired more animators and gave them a budget to create new cartoons. He wasn't really interested in what the animators drew or the stories they came up with as long as the cartoons had plenty of jokes.

"Our policy has always been laughs—the more the merrier," said Schlesinger.

Chuck Jones was one of the talented animators who joined the studio, and he confirmed, "Leon didn't care what we did as long as he got thirty cartoons a year."

Schlesinger was always worried about the Looney Tunes budget. One way to save money was to put the animators to work in a run-down building that was not far from the Warner Bros. studio. The building was in such bad shape that the animators nicknamed it "Termite Terrace."

Artist Bill Melendez recalled that Termite Terrace was not much more than a wooden shack. "The walls were very thin. You could lean on them, and they'd fall apart. The windows had never been cleaned since the building was built. But it had the proper atmosphere for cartoonists."

Because the animators worked on their own,

they were able to have a lot of fun. They started making wild and nonsensical cartoons. The Looney Tunes were very fast-paced and often much funnier than cartoons from other studios. Disney cartoons cost more to produce and had fancier animation, but the Warner Bros. cartoons got more laughs. What the Looney Tunes cartoons lacked was a star.

The 1935 cartoon *I Haven't Got a Hat* is the story of a school recital in the elementary class of a teacher named Miss Cud. She is a cow. One of her students is a kitten named Little Kitty, who performs "Mary Had a Little Lamb." A pair of puppies named Ham and Ex sing the cartoon's title song. But it is another student who steals the show. He is a chubby, stuttering pig named Porky. The other students laugh as Porky nervously tries to recite a poem, "Paul Revere's Ride," and stutters through almost every word of it. Finally, Warner Bros. had their star.

Porky quickly became the most popular Looney Tunes character. By 1936, he was appearing in a new cartoon almost every month.

The animators at Termite Terrace started adding more and more jokes to each cartoon and experimenting with wackier stories. Often, the Looney Tunes characters would pause in the middle of a cartoon and turn to face the audience, as if speaking directly to them. Audiences loved it, and it soon became a regular feature of the Looney Tunes cartoons.

Scene from *Rover's Rival*

In the 1937 cartoon *Rover's Rival*, Porky did more than just talk to the audience. At the end of the cartoon, a cheerful tune called "The Merry-Go-Round Broke Down" was playing. Just then, in the middle of the song, Porky crashed through the movie credits. He waved his pudgy hand in the air and stuttered, "Th-th-that's all, folks!"

For decades after that, almost every Looney Tunes cartoon would end the same way, with Porky sending the audience home laughing.

# Animated Cartoons

There are many steps—and a lot of people—involved in the creation of an animated cartoon. Computers play a big role in the process of making cartoons today, but many of the original steps remain the same.

Artists create a storyboard that looks like a long comic strip from a script showing what happens in the story.

The actors and musicians record the dialogue and music.

Animation artists create the two most important drawings for each scene, called the "extremes." They show the beginning and the end of an action.

Next, an "in-between" artist draws the rest of the art needed to finish the cartoon. Many drawings are often required to create a full scene. For example, it can take up to eight drawings for a character to say "hello" in a cartoon.

A background artist draws all the backgrounds. These include all the settings but not the characters.

When all the pencil drawings are completed, other artists use ink to transfer the drawings to see-through sheets of plastic called cels.

Finally, one cel after another is placed on top of the background drawing, and a cameraperson photographs each one.

After all the cels and backgrounds are photographed, the music and voices are added to the film. The cartoon is finished!

# CHAPTER 4
# A Very Daffy Duck

There were two important additions to the Warner Bros. animation team in the mid-1930s. The first was composer Carl Stalling, who was in charge of writing the music for all the cartoons. Stalling was a very busy man, often composing music for an entire cartoon each week. He wrote new music and also used popular songs and classical themes for the cartoons.

Stalling especially loved to use songs written by a pianist and bandleader named Raymond Scott. Scott sold his songs to Warner Bros. in 1943. They often had ridiculous titles, such as "Celebration on the Planet Mars," "Dinner Music for a Pack of Hungry Cannibals," and "Bumpy Weather over Newark."

Raymond Scott

Another new arrival to the Schlesinger studio was Mel Blanc, who was hired to provide a new voice for Porky Pig in 1937. Blanc kept Porky's stutter, but he also made him much funnier.

# Carl Stalling (1891–1972)

At the age of twelve Carl Stalling played the piano to accompany silent movies at his local theater. He grew up to become an orchestra conductor. And in 1928, he started working with Walt Disney and wrote music for the early Mickey Mouse cartoons. Stalling even once provided the voice of Mickey in a 1929 cartoon.

After leaving the Disney studio, Stalling composed music for the Looney Tunes and Merrie Melodies series of cartoons. From 1936 until his retirement twenty-two years later, Carl Stalling wrote the music for more than six hundred Warner Bros. cartoons!

# Mel Blanc (1908–1989)

Mel Blanc was known as "the man of a thousand voices." He began performing on radio shows at the age of nineteen. He found steady work as a radio performer in Los Angeles in the 1930s, but he really wanted to work in the movies. In 1936, he auditioned for the job of providing a new voice for Porky Pig. Blanc got the job and ended up providing the voices for almost all the major Looney Tunes characters for the next fifty years.

Blanc also worked on cartoons for other movie studios. In the 1940s, he originated the high-pitched voice and laugh of Woody Woodpecker. Decades later, he lowered his voice to portray the grouchy Cosmo Spacely on *The Jetsons*. He was also the voice of Toucan Sam in Froot Loops cereal commercials for many years.

In the 1940 cartoon *You Ought to Be in Pictures*, Leon Schlesinger made a surprise appearance on film to chat with Porky, who humorously stammered, "Hello, Mr. Schle—, Mr. Schle—, hello, Leon!"

Blanc's voice had the ability to bring something new to every character and to create a unique personality for each one. That voice was very important to the success of the Looney Tunes cartoons.

In 1937, a new character challenged Porky Pig's status as the top Looney Tunes star. His name was Daffy Duck, and he made his debut in the cartoon *Porky's Duck Hunt*. The excitable duck introduces himself to Porky with these words: "I'm just a crazy, darn-fool duck!" He then bounces hysterically over a lake and disappears over the horizon, all the while yelling, "Woo-hoo-hoo-hoo-hoo!"

# The Looney Tunes Theme Song

The opening and closing music for the Looney Tunes cartoons was "The Merry-Go-Round Broke Down," a catchy song written by Cliff Friend and Dave Franklin in 1937. Although the cartoon used only the music, the song did have words that began with: "Oh the merry-go-round broke down, as we went 'round and 'round."

In a 1938 cartoon called *Daffy Duck and Egghead*, Daffy sang his own version of the song:

"My name is Daffy Duck.

I worked on the merry-go-round.

The job was swell,

I did quite well,

till the merry-go-round broke down.

Hoo-hoo! Hoo-hoo! Hoo! Hoo! Hoo-hoo!"

Audiences had never seen anything quite like Daffy. Part of his appeal was his silly voice. With the encouragement of the animators, Mel Blanc based Daffy's voice on the speech patterns of Leon Schlesinger! It seemed that the studio head hissed slightly when he spoke the letter "s." So when Daffy called someone "despicable," it came out "dessssss-picable."

Daffy Duck's wild attitude quickly made him the favorite Looney Tunes character. His time at the top would only last a few years, though. An even more popular character was about to hop into the Warner Bros. cartoons.

# CHAPTER 5
## "What's Up, Doc?"

The next big Looney Tunes star was a mischievous gray rabbit who showed up in the 1940 cartoon *A Wild Hare*. You can't exactly call it his debut, because earlier versions of this rabbit had been around for a few years. A 1938 cartoon featured a white rabbit who had a personality very much like Daffy Duck's. This unnamed bunny had a nutty laugh, and he hopped around wildly.

A wild hare becomes Bugs Bunny

He appeared in a few more cartoons, but it wasn't until 1940 that a revised and more final version of the rabbit was ready for stardom.

By then, he had become taller and slimmer, and he no longer seemed so much like Daffy Duck. This smart and sarcastic bunny who arrived in *A Wild Hare* was named Bugs, and the man who gets credit for giving Bugs his look and style was animator Tex Avery.

*A Wild Hare* begins with hunter Elmer Fudd stalking through a forest. Turning to face the audience, Elmer cautions, "Shhh. Be vew-wy, vew-wy quiet—I'm hunting wabbits."

Elmer is successful, but it's no ordinary rabbit that he finds. The first words out of Bugs Bunny's mouth are a sassy "What's up, Doc?" During the entire cartoon, Bugs annoys Elmer. This rascally rabbit twists Elmer's gun into a knot. He kisses the confused hunter on the lips. And when Elmer mistakenly believes that he has killed the rabbit, Bugs gives one of the most dramatic death scenes ever seen in movies.

Finally, Bugs sneaks up behind the hunter to give him a powerful kick in the rear. Elmer admits defeat and wanders off sobbing, "Wabbits! Wabbits!" As Bugs marches away in triumph, it's clear that a cartoon superstar has been born.

# Tex Avery (1908–1980)

Frederick Bean "Tex" Avery was one of the most talented animators and directors at Termite Terrace. He worked for Warner Bros. from 1935 to 1941. His cartoons are known for their nonstop action. He not only directed the first Daffy Duck and Bugs Bunny cartoons, but he was also credited with coming up with the rabbit's most famous line: "What's up, Doc?"

After leaving Warner Bros., Avery moved to Metro-Goldwyn-Mayer (MGM) and formed his own animation unit. There he worked on cartoons featuring Screwy Squirrel and a slow-moving dog named Droopy.

# Who's "Doc"?

Many have wondered where the expression "What's up, Doc?" came from. Why would Bugs Bunny call Elmer Fudd "Doc"? Tex Avery later explained that it was a common expression he heard when he was growing up in Texas. He thought it would be funny for Bugs to use it.

The animators realized that their brash bunny would need some worthy new opponents. One of Bugs's most famous foes was a small and very noisy cowboy named Yosemite Sam. This pint-size, hot-

Yosemite Sam

tempered, "rootin' tootin' shootin'" character was such a hit that he reappeared in later cartoons with new identities, including roles as a medieval knight, Roman gladiator, and pirate captain. Mel Blanc said that Yosemite Sam was the toughest voice to perform: "Imagine screaming at the top of your lungs for an hour and a half."

# Perfecting Bugs

Almost every popular cartoon character changes and develops over time before reaching his or her final form. Bugs Bunny was no exception. This is perhaps why several writers and artists have tried to take credit for his creation. A small, slightly chubby white rabbit appears in the 1938 Warner Bros. cartoon *Porky's Hare Hunt*. This rabbit has a crazy laugh, and he even flies, rotating his ears like airplane propellers. A year later, the rabbit shows up in *Hare-Um Scare-Um* with large buckteeth and fur that was now gray and white.

1938          1939          1940

Animator Chuck Jones used that toothy rabbit in the 1940 cartoon *Elmer's Candid Camera*. For the first time, the rabbit plays a series of practical jokes on the confused character of Elmer Fudd. That same year, animator Tex Avery reunited the rabbit and Elmer in *A Wild Hare*. In this carton, the smart-aleck rabbit is slimmer and looks much more like the Bugs Bunny of today. And, of course, this is the cartoon where Bugs first utters his famous line, "What's up, Doc?" Bugs had arrived.

1942          1957          1996          2010

The Looney Tunes writers and artists matched Bugs Bunny with many creative characters over the years. The whirling, twirling, and growling animal known as the Tasmanian Devil was a spinning tornado of pure energy with a giant mouth. Also known as "Taz," he ate everything in his path. There was the green-skinned Witch Hazel, who only ever wanted to toss Bugs into her big black cooking pot. She grabbed a bottle of poison called arsenic and added it along with a few other ingredients to make a spell, singing, "A cup of arsenic, a spider, and you-ooo."

One of the rabbit's more memorable foes was the tiny space alien with a giant temper named Marvin the Martian. "You have made me very angry. Very angry indeed!" Marvin complained to Bugs. And when Marvin got angry, he would try to evaporate Bugs with his ACME Disintegrating Pistol.

And of course there was Daffy Duck, who always seemed jealous of Bugs's stardom. The two faced off several times, with Daffy trying to outdo his rabbit rival. Bugs managed to win almost every battle with the frustrated duck.

## CHAPTER 6
## New Arrivals

In the 1940s, the Warner Bros. animation studio was one of the most creative places in Hollywood. The writers and artists at Termite Terrace launched more popular cartoon characters than any other studio.

In 1942, a tiny yellow canary with a huge head said, "I tawt I taw a putty tat," in the cartoon *A Tale of Two Kitties*. Within a few years, the bird acquired the name Tweety and was teamed with Sylvester, a black-and-white cat with a big red nose. In cartoon after cartoon, Sylvester repeatedly tried to swallow Tweety, but the clever canary always managed to outsmart the frustrated cat. Sylvester, who sounded a little like Daffy Duck, turned out to be a very popular character. He was often teamed up with other Looney Tunes characters. He had a pint-sized son named Junior.

In 1946, a loud rooster named Foghorn Leghorn appeared as a new Looney Tunes character who made it his mission to boss around all the other animals in the barnyard. Foghorn was a noisy southern rooster who loved to hum the Civil War–era song "Camptown Races." He also found time to teach the barnyard rules to a young hawk name Henery.

Foghorn Leghorn and Henery

Another major Looney Tunes character to arrive in the 1940s was the romantic French skunk named Pepé Le Pew. In the 1949 cartoon *For Scent-imental Reasons*, Pepé falls madly in love with a black cat who has accidentally had a white stripe painted down her back. Pepé thinks she is a skunk and chases her nonstop. Unfortunately for Pepé, the cat is not at all interested in dating this romantic—and smelly—character.

Of course, not every Looney Tunes character was a star. There were a number of characters who didn't quite make it to stardom, but they had their moments of fame. Perhaps the most memorable of these is Michigan J. Frog.

## *One Froggy Evening*

*One Froggy Evening* stars a singing and dancing frog who only ever appeared in this one cartoon. Michigan J. Frog wears a top hat and carries a cane. He's a talented frog, but he will—frustratingly—only perform for his owner. One of his most popular and well-known songs is "Hello! Ma Baby."

This animated short was released in 1955, and nearly forty years later, in 1994, was voted the fifth greatest cartoons of all time.

While these quirky characters were making audiences laugh on-screen, there were two big changes happening behind the scenes at Warner Bros. Tex Avery found a new job and left Termite Terrace. And in 1944, Leon Schlesinger retired.

An executive named Edward Selzer was now in charge of Looney Tunes. He didn't know much about the process of making cartoons,

but he wasn't shy about interfering with the animators at Termite Terrace. Chuck Jones told the story of a time when the writers and artists were having a story meeting. Mr. Selzer entered the room and demanded to know what all the laughing was about. He didn't understand what could be so funny about making cartoons!

# CHAPTER 7
## "Beep! Beep!"

In 1949, animator Chuck Jones introduced two of the most popular Looney Tunes characters. One was a hungry coyote named Wile E. Coyote. The other was the Coyote's favorite food, a fast-running bird known as the Road Runner. Audiences loved the Coyote's crazy schemes to catch the Road Runner, especially because every one ended in disaster for the frustrated Coyote. In the cartoon *To Beep or Not to Beep*, the Coyote builds a catapult that holds a boulder—ready to smash the Road Runner. The giant rock always lands on the Coyote, no matter where he decides to stand. And when the Coyote hides underneath the catapult, it, too, crashes down on top of him.

Chuck Jones created a few rules for the Road Runner series:

- The cartoons always take place in the same desert setting.
- The characters do not talk, except for the occasional "Beep! Beep!" from the Road Runner.
- The Road Runner never leaves the road.
- The Coyote's injuries are always his own fault.
- The Coyote purchases mail-order products

from the ACME Corporation to try to catch the Road Runner.

- No matter how much the Coyote suffers, he always recovers to try again.

As Chuck Jones put it, these cartoons are "not about how many ways you can catch a Road Runner, they're about how many ways you *can't* catch a Road Runner."

# Chuck Jones (1912–2002)

Chuck Jones worked at Warner Bros. for almost three decades. He was responsible for the look and humor of some of the most famous Looney Tunes cartoons of all time. Jones directed his first cartoon in 1938 and, within a few years, had perfected his outstanding talent as both an artist and a storyteller. He also had a great sense of comedic timing, which can be seen most clearly in the Wile E. Coyote and Road Runner cartoons in the 1950s.

After leaving Warner Bros., he worked at MGM, and in 1966, he directed the popular TV adaptation of Dr. Seuss's *How the Grinch Stole Christmas*. Jones's cartoons won three Academy Awards, and in 1996, he received his own honorary Academy Award.

In 1953, the final major Looney Tunes character was introduced. His name was Speedy Gonzales, and he was known as the fastest mouse in all of Mexico. Speedy wore a giant sombrero. He often yelled, "Arriba! Arriba!" which means "Hurry up!" Many different cats chased him, but none of them were quick enough to catch the fast-moving Speedy.

By 1960, nine out of ten households in the United States had television sets. Short films started to disappear from movie theaters as movies began facing competition from television. In 1963, Warner Bros. decided to close its animation studio. But that wasn't the end of the Looney Tunes characters. Soon they found a new home that would make them more popular than ever.

## *So Much for So Little*

In 1949, Warner Bros. released an educational film called *So Much for So Little*. The film was commissioned by the Public Health Service in Washington, DC. The government wanted to show that everyone needs proper health care to survive. The short film presented diseases as monstrous creatures who were just as wild as some of the Looney Tunes characters. *So Much for So Little* became the only cartoon ever to win an Academy Award for best documentary short subject of the year!

# CHAPTER 8
# The Best of the Best

What are the very best Looney Tunes cartoons? Five of them—*Tweetie Pie, For Scent-imental Reasons, Speedy Gonzales, Birds Anonymous,* and *Knighty Knight Bugs*—won the Academy Award for Best Animated Short Film. Another four—*Porky in Wackyland, Duck Amuck, One Froggy Evening,* and *What's Opera, Doc?*—

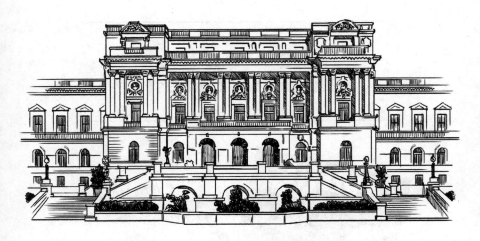

were chosen by the United States Library of Congress to be included in its National Film Registry. Are these the best cartoons of all time? Here are a few of these award-winning stories.

### *Porky in Wackyland* (1938)

This black-and-white cartoon is one of the wildest Looney Tunes cartoons ever. In it, Porky Pig travels to Africa in search of the legendary Dodo bird. A newspaper headline declares that the possibly extinct bird is worth four trillion dollars! Porky arrives in Wackyland, where a sign declares,

"It can happen here. Population: 100 nuts and a squirrel." It turns out that *anything* can happen in Wackyland. Porky meets a peacock with playing cards in place of tail feathers. Another animal has a dog at one end and a cat at the other, and both ends are battling each other. When the Dodo turns up, he has the head of a bird, really big feet, and arms that expand and retract. The Dodo also has the talents of a skilled animation artist. When Porky chases the Dodo, the clever bird takes out a pencil, draws his own door, and escapes through it.

## *For Scent-imental Reasons* (1949)

The French skunk Pepé Le Pew falls madly in love with a cat who accidentally happens to look just like a skunk. In this cartoon, Pepé chases her around a perfume shop in Paris.

When he has the struggling cat locked in his arms, he tries to win her over and says in a thick French accent, "Ah, my leetle darling. It is love at first sight, is it not?" A few minutes later, the tables are turned when Pepé falls into a can of blue paint. His skunky odor is blocked and his stripe has been covered. This time the female cat chases *him*. It turns out that Pepé doesn't like it when he's the one being chased!

## Duck Amuck (1953)

As *Duck Amuck* opens, Daffy Duck thinks he is in a regular cartoon. He is portraying a brave French soldier, waving his sword in the air. Just then, the French countryside behind him disappears, leaving him standing against a white background. "Psst," Daffy whispers. "Whoever's in charge here . . . the scenery! Where's the scenery?" A giant paintbrush quickly provides a new background of a farmyard with a red barn. Daffy's outfit suddenly looks very out of place. He quickly changes into farmer overalls and starts singing, "Daffy Duck, he had a farm." Just as quickly, the background switches to a snowy landscape, then a Hawaiian jungle. When Daffy complains one time too many, a large pencil eraser comes into the scene and erases Daffy!

And who is the animator behind all this confusion? It turns out to be Bugs Bunny at the drawing desk. "Ain't I a stinker?" he says with a smile.

### *One Froggy Evening* (1955)

This is the cartoon starring a singing frog. That's pretty much all you have to tell people to remind them of this hilarious and one-of-a-kind cartoon. It's the story of a construction worker who discovers a singing and dancing frog. The man dreams of becoming rich and famous, and he presents his amazing discovery to the world. Sadly for the man, it's at that exact moment that the frog goes silent. As cartoon historian Leonard Maltin says, "*One Froggy Evening* is one of those miracle cartoons. It came out of nowhere. It was just a simple idea. It was not part of a continuing series.

And yet it's perfect. I think of it as kind of the cartoon equivalent of a really good short story."

### What's Opera, Doc? (1957)

There's never been a cartoon like *What's Opera, Doc?* Bugs Bunny and Elmer Fudd sing music from *The Ring of the Nibelung*, a famous four-part opera by the German composer Richard Wagner. In the cartoon, Bugs tricks Elmer by dressing up as the opera's female star, Brunhilde. When Elmer sees that Brunhilde is actually Bugs, he threatens to "kill da wabbit!" But to be sure that Bugs lives to star in another cartoon, the story ends with him turning to the audience and saying, "Well, what did ya expect in an opera? A happy ending?"

### *Knighty Knight Bugs* (1958)

In this cartoon, King Arthur orders his court jester, Bugs Bunny, to bring him a magical Singing

Sword. Unfortunately for Bugs, that sword is locked up in the castle of the Black Knight. (The Black Knight looks a great deal like Yosemite Sam except that he wears a suit of armor instead of a cowboy outfit.) Bugs manages to grab the sword, but the Black Knight and his fire-sneezing dragon chase him throughout the castle, trying to take the sword away from Bugs. "Drop that sword, Varmint!" yells the Black Knight, and the chase is on. When the Black Knight and his dragon find themselves locked in a storeroom full of dynamite and other explosives, you can probably guess what happens next. The dragon lets out one final fiery sneeze.

# *Duck Dodgers in the 24½th Century*

Although it didn't win an Oscar or make it onto the National Film Registry list, the 1953 cartoon *Duck Dodgers in the 24½th Century* is one of the most beloved Looney Tunes films of all. In 1994, it was voted #4 on a list of the fifty greatest cartoons of all time by members of the animation field.

*Duck Dodgers* is a parody of a popular newspaper comic strip and film series called *Buck Rogers in the 25th Century*.

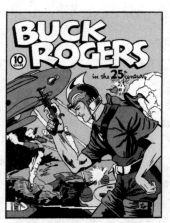

Buck Rogers comic book

Daffy Duck stars as a fearless space hero, and Porky Pig is his eager assistant. Together they travel to Planet X in search of the rare "shaving cream atom." On Planet X, Daffy and Porky meet Marvin the Martian, the hot-tempered space alien who carries a dangerous disintegrator gun.

# CHAPTER 9
## TV Stars

With the cost of making new cartoons rising, Warner Bros. decided to stop creating new ones in the 1960s. But that wasn't the end of Bugs Bunny and his friends.

Decades after Looney Tunes had been shown in movie theaters, the cartoons found a new home. *The Bugs Bunny Show* made its television debut on a Tuesday night in 1960. It was originally shown in black and white. At the beginning of each show, Bugs and Daffy appeared onstage. Together, they danced and sang the catchy theme song "This Is It" with these lyrics: "Overture, curtains, lights! This is it, the night of nights. No more rehearsing and nursing a part. We know every part by heart!"

After that, a parade of Looney Tunes characters danced onstage, from the smallest (Tweety) to the tallest (Foghorn Leghorn). During the show, different Looney Tunes characters appeared as guest hosts in newly animated short segments.

The characters would introduce classic Warner Bros. cartoons and sometimes give a behind-the-scenes look at how those cartoons were created.

Today, there are several animated series airing on television between 8 p.m. and 11 p.m. (also known as "prime time"), but in the early 1960s, watching cartoons in the evening was quite unusual. *The Flintstones* was the first successful prime time cartoon, and it premiered the month before *The Bugs Bunny Show*. Both shows even featured voices by the great Mel Blanc. He created voices for *The Bugs Bunny Show* guest host introductions as well as the voices of Barney Rubble and Dino on *The Flintstones*.

# Bugs and Tex Reunite

In the 1960s, Bugs Bunny battled Elmer Fudd once again in a series of TV commercials for Kool-Aid. The director of those commercials was former Warner Bros. animator Tex Avery, who decades earlier had directed *A Wild Hare*, the first real Bugs Bunny cartoon.

*The Bugs Bunny Show* quickly became a big
hit, both with adults who remembered seeing
the cartoons in movie theaters and with children
who were seeing the Looney Tunes characters for
the first time. The show aired every Tuesday night
at 7:30 p.m. for two years, and then it moved

to Saturday mornings, where it became an even bigger hit. The show continued to air for decades under many different names.

Bugs Bunny and his friends had conquered movies and television. But that's not all, folks. The Looney Tunes characters weren't done yet.

# CHAPTER 10
## Loonier Than Ever

During the late 1960s, Warner Bros. decided to reopen its animation studio. New characters began to appear, including Cool Cat, a tiger with a relaxed attitude who loved jazz music. There was a magical mouse named Merlin. And there were two carrot-snatching rabbits named Bunny and Claude—similar to the real-life bandits Bonnie and Clyde. None of these characters lasted long, but they kept the animators busy.

Warner Bros. animators also produced new cartoons featuring the classic Looney Tunes characters. Bugs Bunny starred in two half-hour TV cartoons, and a series of Road Runner shorts were created in 1971 for the PBS educational series *The Electric Company*.

Bugs Bunny had never starred in a feature film, but that changed in 1975 with the release of the movie *Bugs Bunny Superstar*. It didn't have any new animation, but it featured interviews with the leading Warner Bros. animators and included some of the very best Looney Tunes cartoons from the 1940s and 1950s.

The 1979 movie *The Bugs Bunny/Road Runner Movie*, directed by Chuck Jones, was a collection of some of his classic Looney Tunes cartoons. Jones even gathered together a few of his former workers from Termite Terrace to produce some new animated segments for the movie.

Best of all, in 1980 Chuck Jones got the chance to create a sequel to *Duck Dodgers in the 24$^1$/$_2$th Century.* Daffy Duck, Porky Pig, and Marvin the Martian all returned for the new film, and it was shown during a Looney Tunes Thanksgiving TV special.

# When Bugs Met Mickey

After decades of being stars for their own studios, the Disney and Looney Tunes characters finally appeared together in the Oscar-winning feature film *Who Framed Roger Rabbit*. The 1988 movie blended the live-action of real actors and animation. It tells the story of a private detective who is investigating a crime in Hollywood. The detective travels to Toontown where he meets up with many different cartoon characters.

In their first onscreen meeting, Bugs Bunny and Mickey Mouse team up to annoy the detective. And the world's two most famous animated ducks—Daffy and Donald—give a crazy concert portraying dueling piano players. Daffy gets the last word when he declares, "I've worked with a lot of wise-quackers, but you are *despicable*!"

Over the past few decades, the Looney Tunes characters have stayed busy, and not just in cartoons. In 1987, Bugs Bunny presented the award for Best Animated Short during the Oscars ceremony. And in 1997,

Bugs appeared on a US postage stamp.

The Looney Tunes characters also made regular appearances in the animated series *Tiny Toons Adventures*. That show began in 1990 and featured a new, younger generation of cartoon characters, including Buster Bunny and Plucky Duck, who attended ACME Acres Looniversity. The original Bugs Bunny and his friends were Looniversity professors for the younger characters. Even wild and wacky Daffy Duck became a role model to Plucky Duck.

In 1996, the characters returned to the big screen when they starred opposite basketball legend Michael Jordan in *Space Jam*. The movie was a huge hit and helped to introduce the Looney Tunes characters to a new generation of kids.

*Space Jam* was followed by another live-action and animated feature film in 2003 called *Looney Tunes: Back in Action*. Several famous actors joined the Looney Tunes characters for this movie, including Steve Martin and NASCAR champion racer Jeff Gordon.

Steve Martin in *Looney Tunes: Back in Action*

The story begins on the actual Warner Bros. movie studio lot and features a very frustrated Daffy Duck. After all his years of playing a supporting character to Bugs Bunny, Daffy is fed up. He marches into the head office at Warner Bros. and demands that the executives choose between him and Bugs. Much to Daffy's shock, they choose Bugs. Daffy is fired on the spot!

## *Space Jam*

*Space Jam* tells the story of an evil alien
who decides to kidnap the Looney Tunes characters

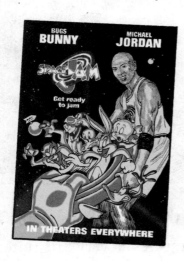

so that he can add them
as a new attraction at
his theme park, Moron
Mountain. Bugs Bunny
challenges the alien
to a basketball game.
If the Looney Tunes win
the game, they get to
go free. The alien agrees
but then steals the powers of top NBA basketball
players for his team. Luckily, Bugs manages to
get some help from Michael Jordan for the Looney
Tunes team.

Michael Jordan had a lot of fun making *Space
Jam*, and he was especially happy that Warner

Bros. built a regulation-size basketball court at the studio for him. It was called the "Jordan Dome," and Michael used it to stay in shape while he made the movie. At the end of each day of filming, he played a ninety-minute game with the other NBA stars of the movie.

In 2010, Wile E. Coyote and the Road Runner entered the digital era in a series of computer-animated 3-D cartoons that were made for movie theaters. Even though he was armed with state-of-the-art 3-D ACME products, the Coyote still wasn't able to catch the Road Runner.

And in 2019, Warner Bros. began producing a new series of short cartoons called *Looney Tunes Cartoons*. Over sixteen hours of new cartoons were made for viewing on TV, the Internet, and even on cell phones. Best of all, the cartoons starred all of the classic characters—including Bugs Bunny, Daffy Duck, and Porky Pig.

It's been a long journey from their humble days in Termite Terrace, but the Looney Tunes characters are still as popular—and appealing—as ever.

# Bibliography

**\*Books for young readers**

Adamson, Joe. *Bugs Bunny: Fifty Years and Only One Grey Hare.*
New York: Henry Holt, 1990.

\*Beck, Jerry. *Looney Tunes™: The Ultimate Visual Guide.* New
York: DK Publishing, 2003.

Beck, Jerry, and Will Friedwald, *Looney Tunes and Merrie
Melodies: A Complete Illustrated Guide to the Warner Bros.
Cartoons.* New York: Henry Holt, 1989.

Feild, Robert. *The Art of Walt Disney.* New York: Macmillan, 1942.

\*Gigliotti, Jim. *Who Was Chuck Jones?* New York: Penguin
Workshop, 2017.

Maltin, Leonard. *Of Mice and Magic.* New York: McGraw-Hill, 1980.

Solomon, Charles. *The History of Animation: Enchanted
Drawings.* New York: Knopf, 1989.

\*Stewart, Whitney. *Who Was Walt Disney?* New York: Penguin
Workshop, 2009.